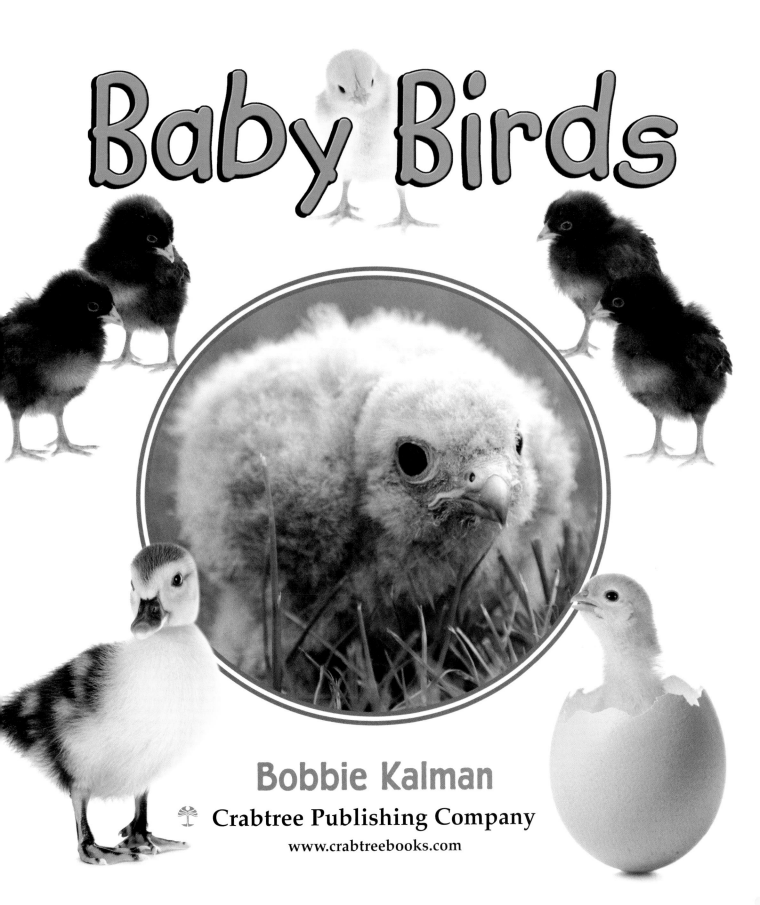

Baby Birds

Bobbie Kalman

🌱 Crabtree Publishing Company

www.crabtreebooks.com

It's fun to learn about Baby Animals

Created by Bobbie Kalman

For sweet Hana Brissenden
You are our family's beautiful princess.
We love you very much!

Author and Editor-in-Chief
Bobbie Kalman

Editor
Robin Johnson

Photo research
Crystal Sikkens

Design
Katherine Kantor
Samantha Crabtree (cover)

Production coordinator
Katherine Kantor

Illustrations
Barbara Bedell: page 21 (top right)
Katherine Kantor: pages 9 (top right and bottom), 24
Bonna Rouse: pages 9 (top left), 11, 23
Margaret Amy Salter: page 21 (bottom left and right)
Tiffany Wybouw: page 16

Photographs
© 2008 Jupiterimages Corporation: pages 20 (top),
  23 (bottom right)
© Shutterstock.com: cover, pages 1, 3, 4, , 5, 6, 7, 8,
  10, 11, 12, 13, 14, 15, 16, 17, 18, 19, 20 (bottom),
  21 (top), 22 (top), 23 (top left), 24 (all except
  top right)
Other images by Corbis, Digital Stock, and Digital Vision

Library and Archives Canada Cataloguing in Publication

Kalman, Bobbie, 1947-
    Baby birds / Bobbie Kalman.

(It's fun to learn about baby animals)
Includes index.
ISBN 978-0-7787-3950-0 (bound).--ISBN 978-0-7787-3969-2 (pbk.)

    1. Birds--Infancy--Juvenile literature. I. Title. II. Series.

QL676.2.K33 2008   j598.13'9   C2008-900469-8

Library of Congress Cataloging-in-Publication Data

Kalman, Bobbie.
    Baby birds / Bobbie Kalman.
        p. cm. -- (It's fun to learn about baby animals)
    Includes index.
    ISBN-13: 978-0-7787-3969-2 (pbk. : alk. paper)
    ISBN-10: 0-7787-3969-4 (pbk. : alk. paper)
    ISBN-13: 978-0-7787-3950-0 (reinforced library binding : alk. paper)
    ISBN-10: 0-7787-3950-3 (reinforced library binding : alk. paper)
    1. Birds--Infancy--Juvenile literature. I. Title. II. Series.

QL676.2.K337 2008
598.13'9--dc22

2008002440

Crabtree Publishing Company

www.crabtreebooks.com   1-800-387-7650

Published in Canada
Crabtree Publishing
616 Welland Ave.
St. Catharines, Ontario
L2M 5V6

Published in the United States
Crabtree Publishing
PMB16A
350 Fifth Ave., Suite 3308
New York, NY 10118

Published in the United Kingdom
Crabtree Publishing
White Cross Mills
High Town, Lancaster
LA1 4XS

Published in Australia
Crabtree Publishing
386 Mt. Alexander Rd.
Ascot Vale (Melbourne)
VIC 3032

What is in this book?

What is a bird?   4

All kinds of birds   6

Bird bodies   8

Bird beaks   10

Bird feet   11

Bird feathers   12

Eggs and babies   14

Inside the egg   16

Time to hatch!   17

Baby bird homes   18

Bird families   20

Bird habitats   22

Words to know and Index   24

What is a bird?

Birds are animals. They are the only animals that have feathers. Birds also have two wings, two legs, and a beak. Most birds fly, but some birds do not fly.

feathers

This bird is a stork. It has two wings, two legs, a beak, and feathers. Storks are birds that fly.

wings

legs

beak

A mother chicken is called a **hen**.

The birds in the picture below are **chicks**. Chicks are baby chickens. Chickens have wings, but they do not fly. Name two other birds that do not fly. See pages 8 and 9 if you do not know.

A father chicken is called a **rooster**.

Most chicks are raised by people. This boy is feeding some chicks.

All kinds of birds

There are many kinds of birds. Birds can be different colors, shapes, and sizes. Some birds are very big. Emus are very big birds. Emus do not fly. They are too heavy to stay up in the air.

These baby emus will grow to be as big as their mother.

Hummingbirds are tiny birds. They flap their wings quickly when they fly.

Woodpeckers make their homes in trees.

Parrots have very colorful feathers.

Gulls live on land. They also fly over oceans looking for fish to eat.

Penguins do not fly. They swim under water in oceans.

Owls are birds called **raptors**. Raptors eat other animals.

Bird bodies

Birds can look very different. The bodies of birds are the same in many ways, however.

The bodies of birds are covered in feathers.

Birds have two wings. Most birds use their wings for flying.

Most birds have eyes on the sides of their heads. They can see around their bodies.

Birds use their beaks for eating food.

Birds walk on two legs.

*Some birds have **claws** on their feet. Claws are sharp, curved nails.*

8

Birds are **vertebrates**. Vertebrates are animals with **backbones**. Backbones are the bones in the middle of an animal's back. The bones of birds are **hollow**, or empty inside. Hollow bones are very light. Light bones help birds stay in the air while they are flying.

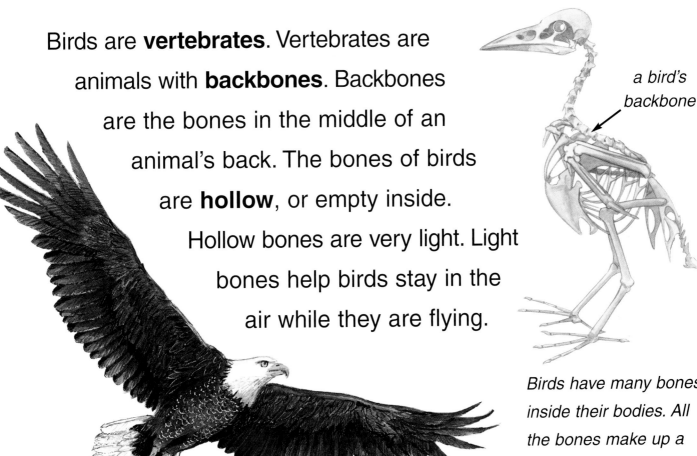

a bird's backbone

*Birds have many bones inside their bodies. All the bones make up a bird's **skeleton**.*

*Birds have **lungs** for breathing air. Lungs are body parts that take in air and let out air. You also have lungs for breathing.*

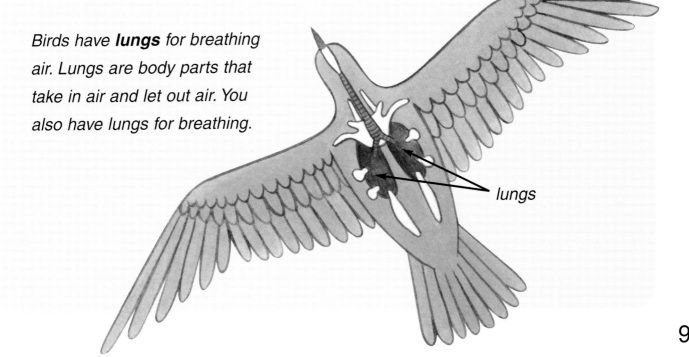

lungs

9

Bird beaks

All birds have beaks. Birds use their beaks to get food or to break it apart. There are many kinds of beaks. The beaks are suited to the ways birds use them.

*Hummingbirds have long, thin beaks for drinking **nectar**. Nectar is a sweet liquid inside flowers.*

Parrots have curved beaks for cracking seeds and biting into fruits.

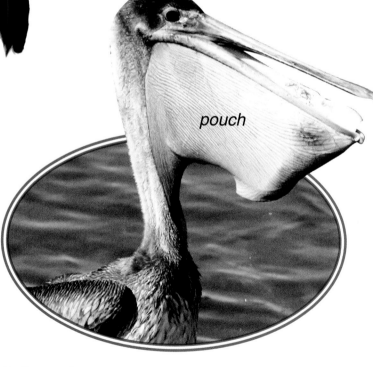

pouch

Pelicans have pouches on their beaks. They fill their pouches with fish. The pelicans then swallow the fish without chewing them.

Bird feet

The legs and feet of birds are different, too. Some birds have **webbed** feet. Webbed feet have skin between the toes. Birds that live on water have webbed feet. Some birds have claws on their feet. Other birds have very long toes.

talons —

*Raptors use their **talons** to catch and hold animals. Talons are sharp, curved claws.*

Ducks live in the water most of the time. Their webbed feet help them swim.

web

Jacanas have long legs and toes. When they spread out their toes, they can walk on plants that grow in water.

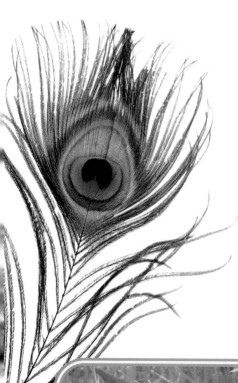

Bird feathers

Birds are covered in feathers. They have soft feathers near their skin. Soft feathers are called **down**. Most birds also have stiff feathers. They use these feathers for flying. Baby birds have only down feathers.

chick

This mother goose has both kinds of feathers. Her baby has only down feathers.

*This chick and **duckling** are both covered in down. A duckling is a baby duck.*

duckling

adult
peacock

baby
peacock

Some birds have brightly colored
feathers. The feathers of adult
peacocks are very colorful, but
the feathers of baby peacocks
are brown. When the male babies
grow up, they will be colorful, too.

*These baby parrots have gray
feathers. They will have red and
green feathers when they grow up.*

13

Eggs and babies

Baby birds are not born. They **hatch** from eggs. To hatch is to break out of an egg. A mother bird first **lays** the eggs. The eggs come out of her body. Baby birds start growing after the eggs have been laid.

This mother swan is turning her eggs to warm the other sides. The eggs must stay warm for the baby birds to grow.

Bird eggs are different colors and sizes. Match the baby birds to the eggs from which they hatched. The answers are shown below.

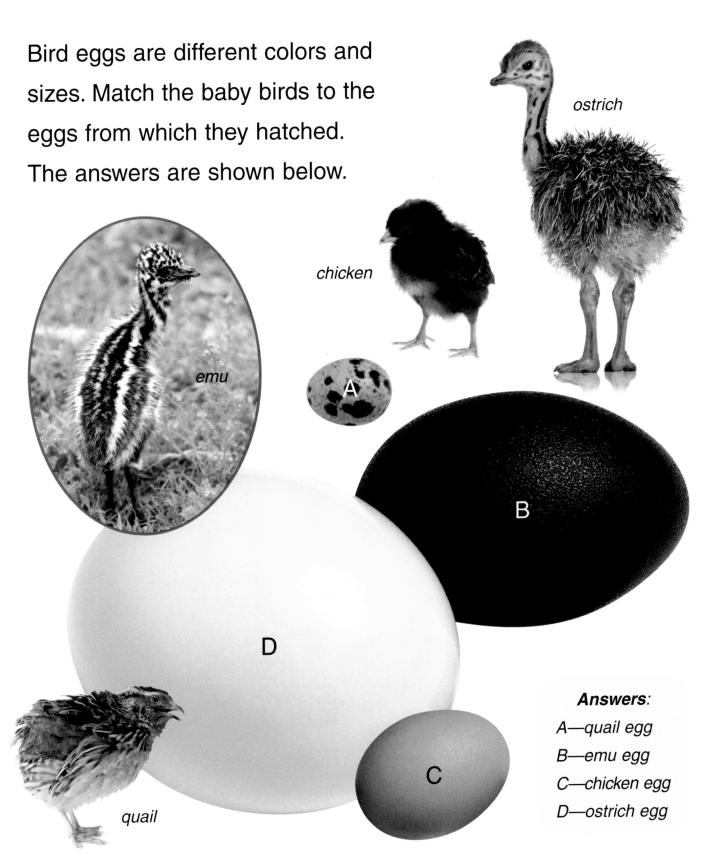

ostrich

chicken

emu

A

B

D

C

quail

15

Inside the egg

Baby birds grow inside eggs. The mother **broods** the eggs. To brood is to sit on eggs to keep them warm. This hen is brooding her eggs. The eggs will take 21 days to hatch.

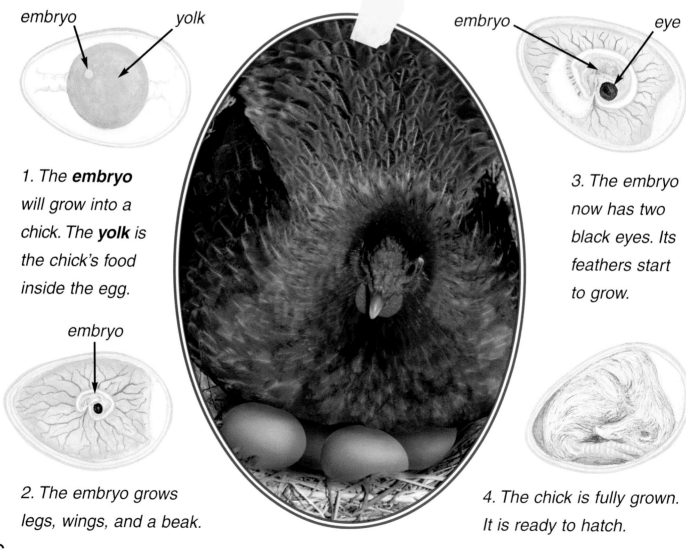

embryo   yolk

*1. The **embryo** will grow into a chick. The **yolk** is the chick's food inside the egg.*

embryo

2. The embryo grows legs, wings, and a beak.

embryo   eye

3. The embryo now has two black eyes. Its feathers start to grow.

4. The chick is fully grown. It is ready to hatch.

Time to hatch!

1. The chick uses its **egg tooth** to break the shell of its egg.

2. It pushes off the top of the egg.

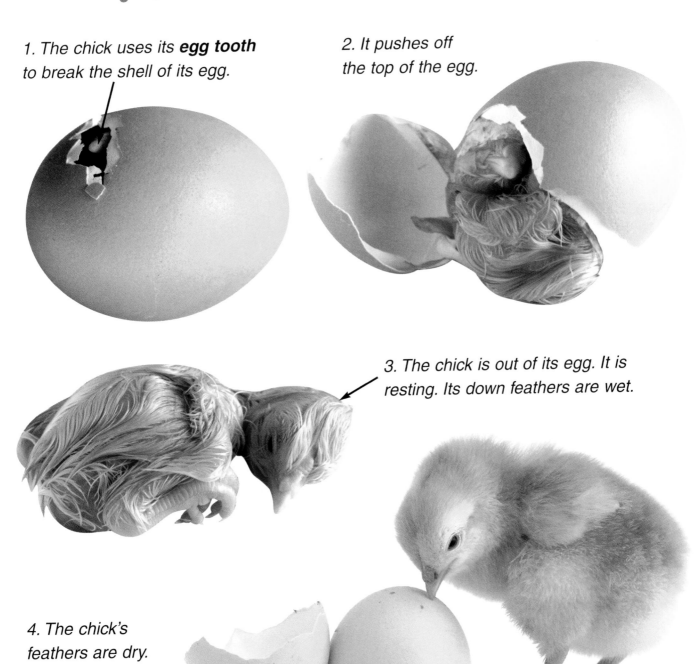

3. The chick is out of its egg. It is resting. Its down feathers are wet.

4. The chick's feathers are dry. The chick is now ready to live outside the egg.

17

Baby bird homes

Many baby birds live in homes called **nests**. Their mothers lay the eggs in the nests. Some babies grow in the nests after they hatch. Nests are made from plants, feathers, and other things.

These penguins are making nests in a large group. The penguins keep one another safe.

moorhen nest

baby starlings

This mother moorhen has made a nest on the water. She is bringing a leaf to add to her nest. These baby starlings are in a nest above the ground. Their nest is high up in a tree. The babies have their mouths open because they are hungry.

Bird families

Mother birds take very good care of their babies. Many father birds also help care for the babies. The fathers bring food and help keep the babies safe. Some father birds look after the babies while the mothers get food.

*These Canada geese parents are swimming with their **goslings**. Goslings are baby geese. Birds that live on the ground or on water learn how to walk and swim right away.*

a mother ostrich and her babies

Several ostrich mothers lay their eggs in one **pit**. A pit is a large hole in the ground. The mothers take turns sitting on the eggs during the day. The fathers sit on the eggs at night. After the babies hatch, both parents look after the baby birds.

a father ostrich

A mother emperor penguin lays one egg. The father takes care of the egg. He keeps it warm inside a pouch over his feet.

The father penguin also keeps the baby warm after it hatches. The mother and father take turns bringing food to the baby.

Bird habitats

parrots

Birds live everywhere on Earth! The natural places where birds live are called **habitats**. These parrots live in a hot **forest** habitat. A forest is a habitat with many trees.

These young burrowing owls and their mother live in a **desert**. A desert is a hot, dry habitat. The owls live in **burrows**, or holes, that are dug by other animals.

Many birds live on water or near water. Other birds fly above water to find food. This duck and her ducklings live on a lake. They find food in the water.

*This baby long-eared owl lives in a **conifer** forest. Conifer forests have trees with cones.*

These baby penguins live in Antarctica. Their habitat is freezing cold! The land and water are covered with snow and ice all year long.

These blue-footed boobies live on oceans, but they lay their eggs on land.

Words to Know and Index

beaks
pages 4,
8, 10, 16

bodies
pages 8-9, 14

eggs
pages 14-17,
18, 21, 23

families
pages 20-21

feathers
pages 4,
7, 8, 12-13,
16, 17, 18

feet
pages
8, 11, 21

flying
pages 4, 5, 6,
7, 8, 9, 12, 23

habitats
pages
22-23

hatching
pages 14,
15, 16, 17,
18, 21

nests
pages 18-19

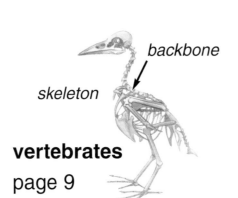

vertebrates
page 9

Other index words
food pages 8, 10, 16, 20,
21, 23
legs pages 4, 8, 11, 16
swimming pages 7, 11, 20
wings pages 4, 7, 8, 16

24

Printed in the U.S.A.